AF414322

A Baby in Heaven's Care

Written by Sydney Lambert

Illustrated by Aamna Ahmad

Big brother
Rusty

To every parent who has longed, prayed, and waited,
this book is for you.

Babies are a true miracle, each one a gift from God. Though our arms are still waiting to hold our rainbow baby, our hearts are filled with hope, knowing that God's timing is perfect. We are deeply grateful for the many people in our lives who continually lift us up in prayer, standing with us in faith for the day our miracle comes.

May this book be a testimony of God's love, a reminder of His promises, and a source of comfort to those who have experienced loss. Even in our grief, He is near. Even in our waiting, He is faithful.

With love and hope, Sydney Lambert

God creates precious little babies and places them in a mommy's tummy,
So small and sweet, growing safe and warm.
When Mommy and Daddy found out, they were filled with joy,
Excited to meet your little sister or brother, whether girl or boy.

We began to dream, to plan, and prepare,
Filling our hearts with love and extra care.
Mommy's tummy would grow, and you'd feel it too—
The joy of knowing someone special was waiting for you.

But sometimes, little babies have to go,
Back to heaven with God, where the angels glow.
We didn't get to meet them, hold them, or play,
But we trust that they're safe with God every day.

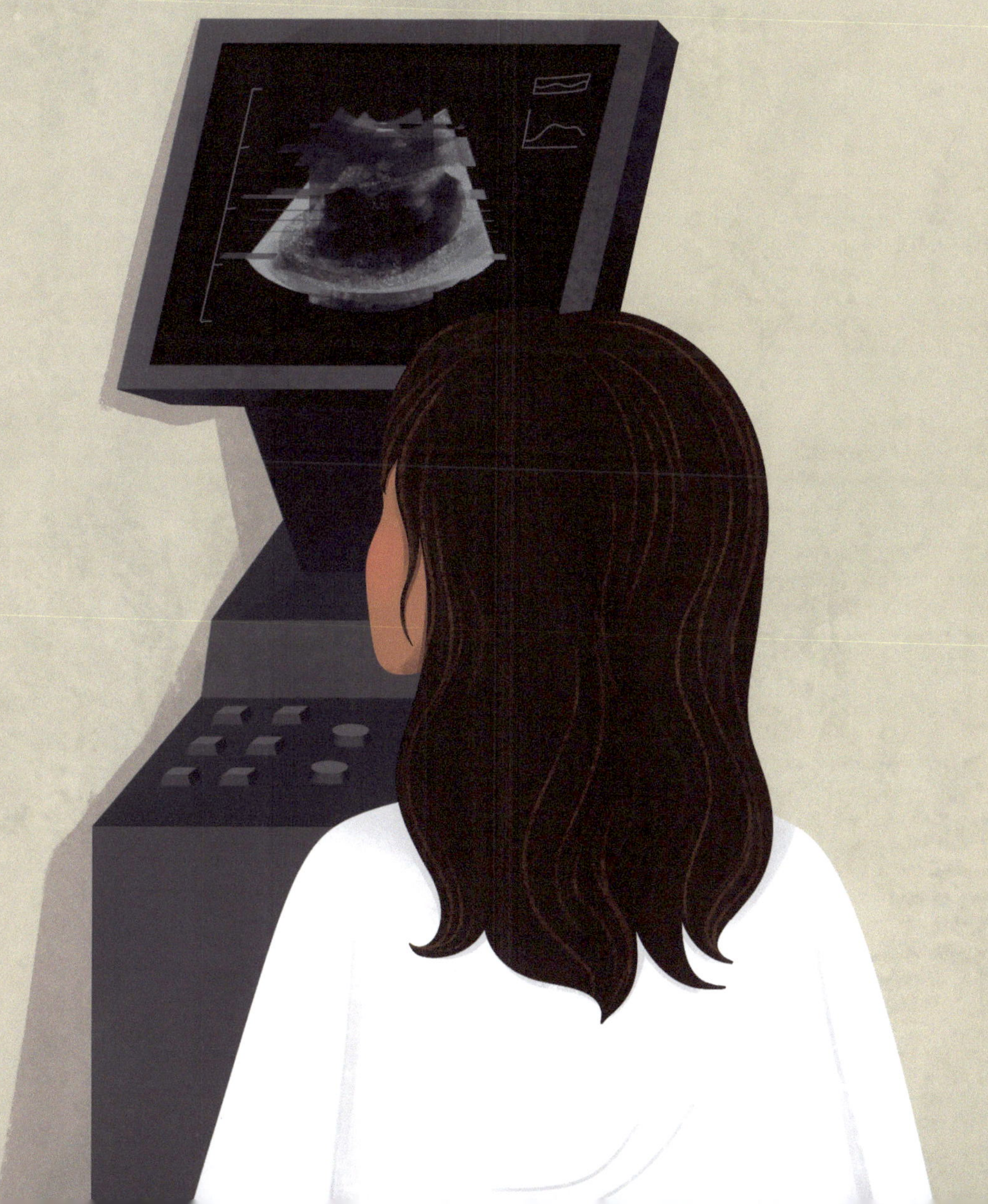

I know you wanted to meet your sister or brother,
To laugh and play, and love one another.
But one day in heaven, you'll see them again,
And we'll all be together, my sweet little friend.

Mommy and Daddy's hearts feel heavy and sad,
We miss your little sibling and the joy we had.
But God gives us strength, with His love so true,
He holds our little baby and watches over you too.

Even though we can't hold them here today,
God has a special place where they'll always stay.
In heaven above, where they laugh and play,
Waiting for us in a bright, beautiful way.

It's okay to feel sad and miss them too,
But know that God's love is holding you through.
He's with us when we smile, and with us when we cry,
Guiding our hearts as the days go by.

Big
Brother

One day, we'll all be together, hand in hand,
In heaven's beautiful and perfect land.
Your sister or brother will be waiting there,
With God's love shining everywhere.

Until then, we carry them in our heart,
Knowing we're never truly far apart.
God's love and His promise will see us through,
Until the day we're all together, us, you, and them too.